Where Does Our Food Come From?

Bobbie Kalman

Dalmatian Press

salid

Created by Bobbie Kalman

Published in 2013 by Dalmatian Press, LLC, Franklin, TN 37068-2068.
1-866-418-2572. DalmatianPress.com

CE16259/1012
Printed in China

Author and Editor-in-Chief
Bobbie Kalman

Educational Consultants
Elaine Hurst
Joan King
Jennifer King

Editors
Kathy Middleton
Crystal Sikkens

Photo research
Bobbie Kalman

Illustrations
Katherine Berti: page 9

Photographs
Comstock: p. 12 (strawberries), 18 (milk and butter)
Photodisc: page 21 (top right)
Other photographs by Shutterstock

What is in this book?

What do you eat?

People eat all kinds of foods.
What foods do you eat?
What foods do you not eat?
Where do foods come from?

grains, bread, pasta

milk, cheese, eggs, meat

fruits and vegetables

Grain foods

We eat foods made from grains every day. Bread, cereal, and pasta are all made from grains.

pizza crust

pasta

cereal

Wheat, corn, oats, and rice are grains. Sometimes we eat grains, like corn and rice, just the way they are.

corn

rice

bread

Growing grains

Grains are the seeds of grasses. Grain plants grow in huge fields.

wheat grains

wheat field

Whole grains contain every part of the grain. They are the healthiest way for us to eat grains.

rice field (paddy)

corn field

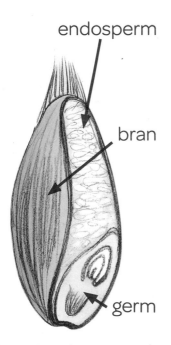

endosperm

bran

germ

whole grain

Vegetables are great!

Vegetables are great for us!
Lettuces, cabbages, beets, and
carrots are some vegetables.
What are your favorite vegetables?

Vegetables are plants grown
for food. We can eat the leaf
(lettuce), stem (celery),
and/or root (carrot).

Some vegetables can be
eaten raw and some
may be eaten cooked.

Fabulous fruits

Fruits contain many things
that our bodies need.
Many fruits taste sweet.
Strawberries taste sweet.

Strawberries
grow in fields.

Fruits come from plants that flower and then produce fruit. Apples, pears, and peaches grow on trees. Bananas, lemons, and oranges also grow on trees. They grow in places that are hot all year long.

Apples grow on trees.

Bananas grow in tropical places.

Help from bees

Did you know that much of the food we eat got help from bees? Bees make plants healthier so they can make a lot of food.

pollen

nectar

Bees fly from flower to flower to collect nectar and pollen. Pollen is a yellow powder plants need to make fruit. Bees take pollen from one plant to another.

Taking pollen from plant to plant is called **pollination**. This bee is pollinating an apple tree.

Sweet tastes

Bees help plants grow, and they also make honey. They make honey from the nectar in flowers. Honey is sweet and yummy!

Another sweet liquid that comes from plants is maple syrup. Maple syrup is made from the sweet sap of maple trees.

Maple sap drips out of a maple tree into a pail. The sap is then boiled until it becomes syrup. Maple syrup tastes great on pancakes!

maple tree

Foods from animals

Meat, milk, cheese, and eggs are foods that come from animals.

Cheese, yogurt, and butter are made from milk. Cows and goats give milk.

cheese

milk

butter

cow

goat

Eggs come
from chickens.

Eggs are a great
breakfast food!

Healthy choices

Some foods are healthier than other foods. Here are some healthy food choices for you.

whole-grain pasta

yogurt

fruits

vegetables

beans

Did you know?

Some vegetables are fruits.
Fruits grow from plants that flower.
Fruits contain seeds.
Tomatoes, peppers, and cucumbers
are just some of the savory fruits
we eat as vegetables. Which other
"veggies" have seeds?

seeds

Index